THE **Credit** *flux*
INSIDE GUIDE TO

credit hedge fund strategies

Credit *flux*
LONDON 2006

The Creditflux inside guide to credit hedge fund strategies

ISBN 1-905450-05-2

Written by Euan Hagger & Dan Alderson

Edited by Euan Hagger

Design & production by Miles Smith-Morris & Roger Thomas

Published by Creditflux Limited
63 Clerkenwell Road, London EC1M 5NP, UK
www.creditflux.com

Contents

You don't need a quant to spell it out for you...

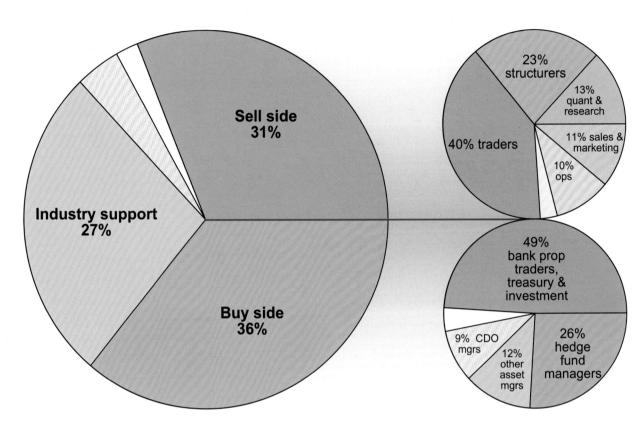

Sell side
31%

Industry support
27%

Buy side
36%

23% structurers

13% quant & research

40% traders

11% sales & marketing

10% ops

49% bank prop traders, treasury & investment

9% CDO mgrs

12% other asset mgrs

26% hedge fund managers

...because the numbers speak for themselves

Chapter 1
introduction:
charting the credit hedge fund universe

The history of the credit derivatives market is the history of credit hedge funds. As the credit derivatives market has grown in depth and complexity, so too has the variety and complexity of strategies that credit hedge funds trade.

A symbiotic relationship is at work. Credit hedge funds, with their active trading styles and eye for untapped sources of value, are natural sources of liquidity. In turn, liquidity provides the building blocks for market development.

For example, the readiness of hedge funds to trade credit correlation dovetailed with the need by dealers to hedge their structured books. This resulted in the emergence of a market for standard index tranches around 2004.

Another example of the beneficial impact of hedge fund liquidity on the market is the emergence of a term structure in credit derivatives. The curve-based investment strategies of long/short funds have played a key part in creating deeper markets outside the five-year point that used to be the only liquid maturity for credit default swaps.

Not only are credit hedge funds natural sources of liquidity, they have been trading in ever increasing numbers. However, estimates of the size of the credit hedge fund market are hard to come by. Some guesstimates suggest that north of $100 billion in assets is being managed across the industry as a whole.

With that growth has come overcrowding. However, hedge funds have a knack for seeking out new opportunities. Unlike active managers of traditional long-only funds, long/short credit hedge fund managers have the freedom to seek out every corner where there is value (see chapter 2). Trading styles are adaptable and, in the case of more esoteric areas such as correlation and volatility, hedge funds can position themselves at the leading edge of product innovation. The fewer other funds that are doing the same, the better.

"Hedge funds will look at whatever opportunities there are to deliver market products that are not generally accessible," says Eric Lepage, global head of structured credit trading and quantitative research at Calyon.

Meanwhile, the pace at which credit hedge fund managers have stepped into new trading strategies and new products is impressive. It helps that some of the brightest sell-side-investment banking professionals now populate the hedge fund industry. It seems a long time ago that hedge funds could simply make money by trading the basis between cash and credit default swaps, based purely on pricing inefficiencies. But in fact it was only a couple of years ago that this was one of the market's biggest opportunities.

Today's list of credit hedge fund trading strategies requires a mini-lexicon. Over the past 12 months, the development of standard ways of trading asset-backed securities and loans in the credit derivatives markets has extended the list further. Major liquidity is predicted from these extensions to cross-asset relative value trading (see chapter 3).

Meanwhile, structured credit hedge funds have been making the most

All in a day's work

The basic definition of a credit hedge fund is simple enough. It is a fund that pursues an absolute return investment objective, in credit or in credit combined with other asset classes. The term "hedge" refers to the practice of covering an investment position (long) with an opposite position (short), in order to reduce or neutralise market risk. The extent to which different funds neutralise market risk varies. Funds that are defined as market neutral may in fact incorporate an element of market risk, or "hidden beta".

Like other hedge funds, credit hedge funds leverage the capital they invest by entering into trades on margin and making use of collateralised borrowing. In some instances, funds may be able to invest without putting up capital initially, but must make margin payments thereafter. A major part of the leverage provided to the fund can come from the repo market via a bank's prime brokerage desk.

In addition, funds can negotiate secured credit lines with their banks, and may even obtain unsecured credit lines.

Ideally, credit hedge funds will look to combine long and short positions to produce positive P&L on day one – through the generation of positive carry. Negative carry will be considered if there is a convincing enough investment case.

The ability to go short as well as long enables hedge funds to exploit a broader range of relative value opportunities than actively managed long-only funds. The result is that credit hedge funds have highly active trading styles, although buy-and-hold strategies also apply.

A hedge fund's absolute return investment objective distinguishes it from a traditional, actively managed long-only fund, which seeks relative returns. A hedge fund aims to deliver a total return that is independent of the general direction of markets: it is unrelated to a benchmark or index. In contrast, in a falling market, a traditional long-only manager would feel justified in delivering a negative return, so long as he beats the benchmark.

At a basic level, therefore, an absolute return credit fund is defined (or should be) by the skills of the manager, and his ability to make effective use of a broader set of trading techniques. By definition, a credit hedge fund should be a cut or two above the rest.

of attractive market conditions (see chapter 4). Following the dislocation in credit correlation in early 2005, correlation funds have acted as a magnet for investment flows, reflecting the fact that correlation looks oversold. Funds have been making the most of the boom times, by rolling out new funds, new strategies and new products.

Other types of institution, such as European and Asian banks, have also been increasing their involvement as direct investors in long/short structured credit plays. For example, equity tranche plays involving selling protection on initial names to default in a broad basket, versus protection buying on initial names to default in a risky sub-basket, form part of the menu of new structures.

Says Lepage at Calyon: "Structured credit long/short strategies used to be more exclusively a hedge fund type play. But there has been a huge increase in other types of investors who are open to the idea and happy to take positions in long/short tranche trades. That can be done synthetically or in funded format, and combined with capital protection."

Adds Lepage: "Correlation is now more demystified, as a result of education, the greater availability of pricing models, and consensus about using base correlation for quoting implied correlation."

One credit hedge fund management firm that trades pretty much the entire gamut of strategies is BlueMountain Capital Management. For starters, the firm is a major participant in the correlation market – and counts early pioneers of credit correlation from the sell side on its staff.

"There is a still a huge amount of potential in correlation strategies," says Andrew Feldstein, CEO and senior portfolio manager, BlueMountain Capital Management. "For example, there has been demand for several billion dollars-worth of equity tranche risk, just from a few months of leveraged super-senior being printed. Correlation is continuing to offer some of the best opportunities in credit, provided you have sophisticated investors who understand that this can be a volatile strategy."

Besides correlation, which has produced a range of BlueMountain standalone funds, the firm pursues six strategies in its flagship multi-strategy fund, the BlueMountain Credit Alternatives fund.

Says Stephen Siderow, president, BlueMountain Capital Management: "We divide the strategies into long/short credit, or inter-credit; intra-credit, which is strategies like curve trading and capital structure trading; index arbitrage – namely, index versus constituents and the indexes against each other; credit volatility, which is directional or relative value; and macro, which includes a variety of broad hedges."

Meanwhile, BlueMountain recently carved out an equity alternatives fund from the equity strategy pursued in the multi-strategy fund.

One investment management firm that has moved in lock-step with the development of the whole market is Stamford, Connecticut-based Aladdin

'Hedge funds will look at whatever opportunitiies there are to deliver market products that are not generally accessible'

Prime brokerage: facing the funds

Innovation in prime brokerage mirrors innovation in credit hedge fund trading. Cleverer trading strategies encourage cleverer financing solutions. It is also a mirror of the credit hedge fund market's full throttle growth. Doing prime brokerage in a relatively new and rapidly expanding market encourages creative thinking.

That can be a cause for celebration, but is also the sort of thing that regulators fret about. The move towards cross-portfolio margining is a case in point. A portfolio-wide, cross-asset approach to funding, as opposed to a product-by-product method, is expected to become standard. It provides benefits to credit hedge funds, as offsetting positions increase the scope to reduce margining requirements. Some prime brokers are even providing cross-entity margining – the margining is based on the business across the entire fund management firm rather than across the products traded by a particular fund.

But with that come risks. For example, regulators worry that cross-asset margining activity might lead to assumptions about correlations, between different positions and strategies, that could prove unreliable in a crisis. It can also entail prime brokers entering into arrangements that involve underlying master trading agreements that differ in areas such as event of default, cure periods and close-out procedures.

The practice of entering into "give up" agreements further complicates the prime brokerage picture. When entering into a "give up", the fund executes at a price supplied by an executing dealer, but then faces the prime broker as counterparty. The prime broker mirrors the transaction with the executing broker as counterparty, thereby intermediating between the two. For the hedge fund, "give ups" make it easier to trade with multiple dealers, allowing for more efficient trade execution. However, that requires the operational capability to monitor and track the more complex flow of transactions. Moreover, poorly defined agreements can introduce the risk of non-acceptance by the prime broker, particularly as products grow more complex.

Isda has responded to this by introducing a master agreement for prime brokerage "give ups". The agreement defines when the prime broker is legally obligated to trade with the fund, and the trading limits applicable to the prime broker's relationship with the fund. The agreement, which was introduced in November 2005, covers interest rate, credit and FX derivatives.

Meanwhile, banks that do not offer prime brokerage are looking to maximise the efficiency of their credit lines. Considerable resources are being devoted to counterparty risk management, and to the development of systems to support netting of long and short positions. Calyon is one bank that is developing new counterparty risk management tools, to help funds gain greater access to its structured credit platform.

Says Eric Lepage, global head of structured credit trading and quantitative research at Calyon: "Counterparty risk – the return versus the cost of line and the volatility of NAV – is a key driving factor of the economics for the hedge fund industry. Netting long and short positions (through VaR or Monte Carlo methodologies) in the counterparty risk computation reduces the amount of line used for a given hedge fund counterparty. We are actively working on the platform we offer to hedge funds, to facilitate their access to our strategies."

Novations are a way of reducing counterparty risk exposure, notes Lepage. "If the hedge fund is remodelling its portfolio of deals facing Calyon, to reduce the tail risk of such a portfolio and its potential drift in PV, that allows us to convince our risk officers that exposure is more limited than it used to be," he says.

"For example, a hedge fund might be selling us some equity protection and buying some mezzanine protection from another dealer to get a global delta neutral position. Instead of each dealer having a large 'risky' position in terms of counterparty risk (because of volatile PV of the deal), a novation of the second leg of the deal to the first dealer would allow him to reduce the value at risk of the elements of the CSA [collateral support agreement] and therefore the counterparty risk."

Capital Management. "We started in 2000, so we count ourselves as one of the pioneers in using credit to generate alpha," says George Marshman, chief investment manager at Aladdin Capital. "Five or six years ago credit was just part of your beta. Alternatives in credit were more or less limited to buying a tranche of a CDO. We were an early adopter of the idea that you can employ leverage, and focus very actively on relative value from both the long and short side."

Adds Marshman: "Some volatility has recently returned, which is welcome as every strategy feeds off volatility. Without that it has been a challenging environment. Investors have really been focusing on performance. But as a fund manager, if you are patient, the market gives you the opportunities to make your returns each year. In 2005 it was the widening of General Motors and Ford and the correlation meltdown. That was a big opportunity."

Delivering outperformance in low volatility hasn't been the only challenge facing hedge fund managers. Some firms are taking the lead in trading systems and operational management – key areas for a market that has grown rapidly, and is trading ever more complex products.

George Marshman, Aladdin Capital Management: we were an early adopter of the idea that you can employ leverage, and focus very actively on relative value from both the long and short side

Hedge fund managers are not necessarily known for prioritising technology infrastructure. However, large funds in particular are channelling significant resources into the systems and operational areas. Some of the biggest IT spends are reported to be taking place at large North American credit hedge fund managers in the correlation market.

Some funds are opting to manage functions in-house that traditionally would have been managed by a prime broker, or fund administrator. "The newer credit funds tend to like to keep the whole process in-house rather than outsource to the prime broker or hedge fund administrator," says a trading systems and derivatives consultant working in this area. "For instance, P&L reporting always used to be a function of the fund administrator. But if you have your own pricing in-house you can create flash P&Ls throughout the day to understand how the portfolio is reacting. That is a big advantage, although a big technical spend is needed."

Credit prime brokerage firms are also responding to operational management challenges. Prime brokerage – the financing and support services provided by banks to hedge funds – is evolving as rapidly in credit as the market it serves (see box on page 8).

In response to the proliferation in products and asset classes that long/short funds trade, prime brokers are offering new brokerage models.

For instance, there is a trend towards cross-portfolio netting for margining (the amount of collateral that hedge funds pay when entering and maintaining trades). But that raises risk management and operational risks that the market must manage effectively.

Meanwhile, the recent introduction of standard market practice for novations – the transfer of existing trades to allow a hedge fund or other counterparty to face a new dealer counterparty – has been central to the credit derivative market's effort to reduce build-ups of unconfirmed trades. As active traders, credit hedge funds make active use of novations, and have been one of the focal points for post-trade processing reforms.

As part of that push, new automated post-trade processing solutions are being funnelled towards long/short funds.

Perhaps ironically, just as large numbers of hedge fund managers have moved into credit, the market has stubbornly failed to produce the volatility on which most trading strategies thrive. Credit spreads have been grinding relentlessly tighter, and the market seems capable of shrugging off even the direst company-specific news.

Life has been looking up recently, with a sharp up-tick in spreads in May 2006, but for much of the first part of 2006, trying to run a net short strategy has been a trying experience.

The script was supposed to read a little differently. Limited upside to corporate spreads and rising event risk suggested that the short side of the market was the place to be. In fact, the upside to corporate spreads proved to be extraordinarily elastic, as the floor to credit spreads slowly crumbled before giving way, taking some unwary short traders with it, in March and April 2006.

A series of crunches tighter left some funds feeling the pain. A tangle of factors contributed to the move, according to dealers. A surge in structured credit business, as a result of changes by Standard & Poor's to its rating methodology for CDOs, played a large part.

"Spreads were impacted by the whole CDO market. The change to the rating methodology made it easier to issue additional CDOs," says Wei Foong Lee, joint head of structured products at fixed income credit investment manager BlueBay Asset Management.

Spreads tightened as dealers sold credit protection to hedge the upsurge in CDO issuance.

In addition, panic surrounding event risk trades contributed to the tightening, particularly in the European market.

Event risk trades – particularly plays which look to profit from the leveraging up of company balance sheets as a result of leveraged buy-outs and other M&A activity – have recently been among the most popular credit hedge fund strategies (see chapter 6).

The private equity market is awash with liquidity, and aggressive terms are available. For long/short funds, it has therefore seemed a relatively simple matter of picking the right companies, waiting for acquisitions (rumours can also do the trick) and making money as spreads widen to reflect lower creditworthiness.

But there has been a snag. Successor event language – a mechanism for determining which obligations are deliverable into credit derivative contracts following debt reorganisations – has a relatively limited application. The mechanism caters for situations where existing debt is transferred to new borrowers, for instance after mergers. In those instances, existing credit derivative contracts move to the new reference entities.

But the mechanism does not cover other situations, such as when debt is bought back and new debt is issued in a new entity isolated from the previous entity. In those instances, buyers of protection can look forward to holding positions that are in effect of no value, as their trades no longer reference any debt.

Recent M&A activity has provided plenty of situations where that may apply. Loss of confidence in the ability of event risk trades to deliver profits coincided with the technical spread tightening, resulting in a capitulation in these trades.

Meanwhile, curve steepeners got battered as spreads were crushed tighter. Steepeners get used in a variety of contexts – including as a play on LBO names, or simply to capture the steepness of curve shapes, without necessarily too much thought to fundamentals.

Curve steepeners have featured heavily in hedge fund portfolios for long periods since 2004, when steepness in credit curves first started to become pronounced.

However, the big moves tighter in March and April quickly ate into the breakeven cushions for many steepeners, resulting in a scramble for the exit.

Towards mid-May, markets were trying to move the other way, following sharp stock market falls and US inflation panic. Some dealers were saying they had detected some fixed income investors moving into safer asset classes such as asset-backed securities and bank loans, and away from CDOs. That

Wei Foong Lee, Blue Bay Asset Management: spreads were impacted by the whole CDO market. The change to the rating methodology made it easier to issue additional CDOs

will be good news for long/short funds in the flow market, if it helps relieve the technical pressure on spreads from structured credit.

"Although CDOs will continue to contribute to a tight spread environment for the short term, spreads won't stay tight for ever," says Lee at BlueBay Asset Management. "We have been seeing a lot more volatility and positioned ourselves accordingly. It is harder to outperform in an up market. Our type of alpha comes from fundamental credit selection, so it is in down markets that we tend to distinguish ourselves the most."

Chapter 2

new opportunities, new minefields:
curve and basis flow trading

When the carry suddenly goes to pot and there's not enough slide to compensate, it's a curve trader's worst nightmare. That was more or less the situation for traders tempted to hold record steep curve steepeners, going into April 2006.

Curve steepeners have provided reasonable returns for longish periods since 2004, making the trade a popular credit hedge fund strategy. Recently, European curves in particular have offered attractive trading opportunities, due to pronounced steepness. However, traders got crushed in the scramble for the exit, after curves peaked in March. "Steepeners have been a very crowded trade. If you held on too long you got hurt in April. It was the unwind of that trade when people got hurt," says a London-based long-short credit fund manager.

Typically, curve steepeners are constructed as three- to seven-year trades, or five to 10-year trades. Protection is sold in the three- or five-year maturity, and long protection is put on in the five- or 10-year maturity. The bet is that the spread differential between the two points will diverge. Curve flatteners involve buying protection at the shorter-dated maturity, and selling protection at the longer-dated point. The bet is that the spread differential will converge. (see box on page 14).

The slide in question is the return generated in the current curve environment by simply sitting in curve steepeners and watching the passage of time. Also called rolldown, the effect is a natural result of upwardly-sloping curves. For example, there will be a beneficial mark-to-market effect for a five-year trade put on at, say, 100bp, which rolls down the curve and a year later is paying 100bp, when the four-year spot level is 90bp. The steeper the curve, the greater the slide.

Curve flatteners also produce positive rolldown when curves are upwardly sloping – but at the long end of the curve. But it is curve steepeners that have offered the most attractive rolldown, due to pronounced steepness at the front end of the curve. "Most steepener trades take advantage of the extreme rolldown between the four-year and five-year part of the curve," notes a London-based trader.

Rolldown has proved irresistible for credit hedge funds. For example, it

'Playing the skew and looking at theoretical-to-traded is for the more sophisticated players. At an absolute skew level of five basis points, a skew trade becomes attractive'

provided good returns for funds trading European curves over the first part of 2006. Says Aldous Birchall, head of credit index trading at Royal Bank of Scotland in London: "Everyone did well that bought 5–10s curve steepeners as a way of being short, not paying carry and benefiting from the rolldown. Spread compression in the five-year part of the curve going into the March roll was brutal, further enhancing this trade."

While European curves have displayed extreme steepness, North American 5–7 and 7–10 curve shapes stayed largely unchanged over the first quarter of 2006 – but still steep by historical standards.

Although greater steepness is good for slide, there is a trade-off in the form of the carry. Without any duration weighting, curve steepeners are negative carry trades. Duration weighting turns the position into a positive carry trade (more protection is sold than is bought), and in addition reduces the exposure to parallel shifts in the curve, while not eliminating it entirely.

If curves move sharply steeper, the positive carry for new trades can be eroded to such an extent that the economics for curve steepeners start to look suspect.

Tracking curves

Curve steepeners can be viewed either as bullish trades on near-term default risk, or as bearish trades designed to capture spread widening.

The combination of a long and short position hedges steepeners and curve flatteners against parallel shifts in the curve. However, large parallel shifts in the curve can turn positions into a loss.

Curve trades generate slide or positive rolldown, when curves are positively sloping. However, curve steepeners have typically offered more attractive opportunities for slide, because curves have usually been steepest at the front end (where the trader is long risk).

The move towards pronounced curve steepness in the credit markets since 2004 has partly reflected fundamentals. Low historical default rates provide comfort to holders of shorter-dated credit risk, pushing spreads tighter at the front of the curve, but leave uncertainty over longer-dated risk.

However, technicals have increasingly accounted for curve steepness. Partly, that is because curve steepeners have been self-fuelling trades. The more credit protection that is sold at the front end, the greater the tightening pressure at that point becomes.

In addition, the structured credit market has been a major factor in determining curve shapes. Large-scale protection selling at the five-year point, due to dealers hedging their structured books, can push curves sharply steeper. As the term structure in structured credit has been extended, CDO volumes can also help to flatten curves, due to seven-year or 10-year protection selling.

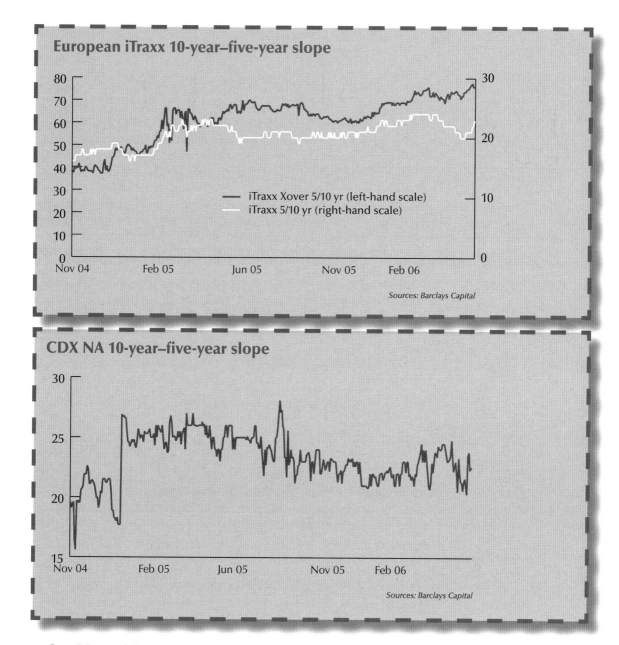

European iTraxx 10-year–five-year slope

iTraxx Xover 5/10 yr (left-hand scale)
iTraxx 5/10 yr (right-hand scale)

Sources: Barclays Capital

CDX NA 10-year–five-year slope

Sources: Barclays Capital

Says Marcus Schüler, head of integrated credit marketing at Deutsche Bank: "You can reach thresholds where a new steepening trade will actually be carry neutral. For example, by the start of March, the positive carry was starting to look fairly marginal." By that stage, the 5–10-year iTraxx Xover curve, for instance, was trading north of 70bp.

When credit markets went on to rally across the curve, curve flattening and the absolute level of spread tightening demolished steepeners.

The fact that a big move tighter started around the time that the credit derivative indices were rolling is no coincidence. The rollovers – six-monthly rebalancings when names drop in and out of the new index series – are a period of high activity for the credit derivatives market.

Dealers say that the short side of the market was already starting to fray, due to CDO-related protection selling, and an unwinding of LBO trades following successor event panic. Deciding whether or not to reset short positions at the rollover wasn't difficult.

Says a senior portfolio manager at a London-based credit hedge fund manager: "When the market went tighter, people were short, and the last thing they wanted was to put on more shorts. Everyone was hitting the bids and taking profits. March saw an unbelievable gapping in – it was another way of playing hidden beta."

The high levels of activity around the rollovers, and the technical factors tied up with the introduction of new index series, make index rollovers a natural point of focus for hedge fund trading. As well as providing opportunities to put on curve trades, rollovers are usually a good time to trade the index basis, or skew.

The index basis is the difference between the index spread and the theoretical spread, derived from the names that constitute the basket. Positive index basis

Back to basis

Different index series tend to display either positive or negative basis, but rollovers introduce volatility to the pattern.

The basis will reflect the market use of the index. For example, if idiosyncratic risk is present, as was the case with the iTraxx HiVol Series 4, the pattern was for hedge funds to go long the index, to finance short positions in individual names.

As a result, the index basis tended to be negative (trading tighter-to-theoretical due to the concentration of long risk positions in the index).

In contrast, the iTraxx Xover index typically gets used by a broad range of traders, including cash-based investors, who want to express a general short position in credit while taking risk in individual companies. The index has therefore tended to trade with a positive basis.

Rollovers add a new dimension to how the basis trades. In theory, the basis will tighten if the index trades with a positive basis, as investors take off short positions ahead of resetting them in the incoming index series. Conversely, protection sellers may want to act in advance, on the view that protection will cheapen up in the incoming series. Expectations that the outgoing iTraxx Xover index would tighten at the five-year point was an argument for putting on curve steepeners going into the March 2006 roll.

More obscure technical factors have also contributed to a loose pattern of indices rallying into the roll, and widening afterwards. Minor mispricings of curve adjustments for the six-month longer on-the-run maturity can make it more attractive for sellers to be in the off-the-run index, to capture rolldown.

means the index is trader wide-to-theoretical, while an index that is trading through theoretical spreads is negative basis.

Trading the index basis, on the view that the basis will revert closer to zero, entails selling or buying protection on the index, and buying or selling protection on a selected basket of names in the same maturity. Thus, trading positive index basis entails going long index risk (the index appears to be trading too wide) and buying protection in names that the investor is bearish on.

Trading the index skew is a popular strategy with some types of long/short credit funds. Often there might be only a couple of basis points of relative value, so it entails trading in size.

Says Paola Lamedica, relative value strategist at BNP Paribas: "Playing the skew and looking at theoretical-to-traded is for the more sophisticated players. At an absolute skew level of 5bp, a skew trade becomes attractive."

Arbitraging the skew between the individual components and the five-year HiVol and main indices is one of the most frequent examples of skew trading that Lamedica says she has seen in the market.

Theoretically, investors could execute arbitrage trades between the index and all the constituents, but that would pile on the transaction costs.

"Structuring the trade using a selected basket of names reduces transaction costs, and combines a view on the basis with a bottom-up view on the individual names," says Tim Backshall, chief credit derivatives strategist at Credit Derivatives Research, an independent credit research house.

Andrew Feldstein, BlueMountain Capital Management: We have dedicated a fair amount of effort to index arbitrage. You have to be able to accommodate a large volume of trading

"We have dedicated a fair amount of effort to index arbitrage," says Andrew Feldstein, CEO and senior portfolio manager at BlueMountain Capital Management. "You need infrastructure for this strategy. You have to be able to accommodate a large volume of trading. The biggest risk is operational risk. You have to be operationally excellent."

Trading indices against each other – for example, selling protection on CDX main and buying protection on CDX Xover – is another source of relative value. Hedge funds also trade the indices against other asset classes, to express macro views. For example, buying protection on iTraxx HiVol and going long equity was a trade executed by some funds early in 2006.

The trade expressed a bearish view on the idiosyncratic risk contained in the index series. On the other side of the trade, equity prices should respond well to an underperforming company that is bought out. It wasn't a trade that necessarily worked well, as buy-out activity was relatively subdued.

Anatomy of a trade

LBO rumours around hotel group Hilton provided good opportunities to execute an event risk basis trade. Henderson Global Investors' credit hedge fund was among the long/short funds that traded the name at the time.

The fund bought 7.125% 2012 sterling-denominated Hilton bonds, at 250bp over the 5% 2012 UK gilt, and sold the underlying government bond on a duration-weighted basis to cancel out the interest rate risk. The fund bought five year euro-denominated credit protection on Hilton at 213bp.

"Often enough an LBO rumour is enough to push the market," says Patrick McHugh, credit trader at UK-based Henderson Global Investors. "There is strong covenant protection on the bonds, so we were looking at an outperformance of the cash bond in Hilton Group versus the CDS. We reasoned that if there was an LBO, they would buy the bonds out."

Adds McHugh: "There was a strong bias towards hoping that the strong covenant protection on the bonds would compress spreads. If the bond spreads were to widen, theoretically I could have lost money. Usually there is a bullish and bearish case to these relative value trades."

Rumours of private equity interest in Hilton's betting business, Ladbrokes, duly surfaced.

"The rumour was enough to drive the market," says McHugh. "There was a flurry of buying activity in the Hilton bonds. At the trade close I sold them at 190bp over. I closed my CDS trade at 181bp, which lost me 32bp, so net-net my profit was 28bp on the trade. It was quite a good pick-up – it was a great relative trade."

Meanwhile, McHugh says food service company Compass provided an attractive opportunity for a curve steepener, earlier in 2006. "There was a drip of bad news in Compass at the time, and we thought CDS was far too tight," he says.

"Between five-year and 10-year we considered the spread was too flat. We thought there was more poor news flow to come."

The fund sold five-year credit protection on Compass at 63bp and bought 10-year protection at 93bp, on a spread DV01-neutral basis. "The news flow did pan out and the curve steepened," he says.

"We bought back the protection in five-year at 118bp, so lost 55bp, but on the flipside we sold 10-year at 157bp – a 64bp profit.

Adds McHugh: "On that trade we actually closed the trade and then went short. We bought five-year protection and made money on the bond directionality as well."

Another relative value trade has been to trade CDX against European iTraxx – to express a view on the relative richness or cheapness of credit in the two markets.

Another strategy is to trade a single name versus the index. For example, if a name is trading tight to the index, and there appears to be little upside to the credit story, selling protection on the index funds a short exposure.

LBO names received a fair amount of this treatment in the first part of 2006. But the trade can apply to any situation where a company's spreads are expected to widen – for example, if it is expected to post poor financial results.

This sort of fundamentals-driven long/short trading can be applied using many strategies, such as name-versus-index, curves and in the case of recent trading of LBO names, the cash-credit default swap basis.

Name-versus-name trading is another frequently applied strategy. The auto sector accounts for some of the most active name-versus-name trading. "We always have a position on in the GM and Ford complex – GM versus GMAC, or Ford versus FMCC," says Feldstein at BlueMountain Capital. "We monitor those all the time and switch it around. There are also opportunities in the auto suppliers – trading the weak names versus the strong names."

Marcus Schüler, Deutsche Bank: Negative basis situations have increased again, as bonds have cheapened up versus CDS

Meanwhile, trading the cash-credit default swap basis no longer has the appeal it had when the cash and credit derivatives market were less efficiently connected. The strategy traded those inefficiencies away.

However, trading in LBO names is being called the new basis trade. The strategy involves buying short to medium-dated bonds that are likely to be bought back in the event of a leveraged acquisition, and buying protection. The trade is that the bonds will be taken out, as banks lending to a leveraged acquisition will not want the bonds paid out in front of them. The bonds should therefore rally, while the credit default swap spread should widen.

However, classic trading of the bond-credit default swap basis is today generally low key. Says Schüler at Deutsche Bank: "Basis trading is a very established business today, and precisely for that reason it has become less interesting. There are so many buyers out there that any proper negative basis opportunity is just snapped up within a matter of minutes. However, recently

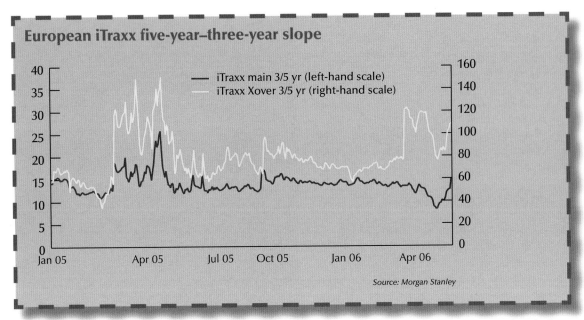

European iTraxx five-year–three-year slope

iTraxx main 3/5 yr (left-hand scale)
iTraxx Xover 3/5 yr (right-hand scale)

Source: Morgan Stanley

the number of negative basis situations has increased again as bonds have cheapened versus CDS."

The credit default swap basis is the difference between the credit derivative spread and the asset swap spread for a given maturity. Negative basis is when the credit default swap premium is tighter than the asset swap yield, and is the basic long/short trade, as it generates positive carry.

Names that have attracted decent volumes of credit default swap basis trading in recent months include RadioShack. Credit derivative spreads and cash market prices became unhinged on the North American electronics retailer in March 2006, generating a negative basis trade. "There was a lot of people chasing that trade," says Backshall at Credit Derivatives Research. Correctly catching the move in RadioShack's basis delivered around 25bp for the trade, over the space of a week.

'We always have a position on in the GM and Ford complex – GM versus GMAC, or Ford versus FMCC'

Chapter 3
broadening the asset mix:
cross-asset relative
value trading

Once upon a time there was a clever trick involving capturing volatility and income from a convertible bond's imbedded equity option and bond component. There still is, barring a bit of a nosedive in 2004 and 2005. Convertible bond arbitrage paved the way for debt-equity capital structure arbitrage proper. But that's only the beginning of the story.

Today, capital structure arbitrage and cross-asset relative value trading is continuing to extend its reach. Equity variance swaps are adding spice to debt-equity relative value trading. Meanwhile, standardised credit derivatives documentation is bringing secured loan assets into the equation for the first time. Similarly, standard confirms for single-name structured finance default swaps is a boost for relative value trading of ABS against other asset classes. There's even a new credit derivatives market in North American preference shares, after dealers got behind a standard confirm developed from a Lehman Brothers' prototype.

Inter-dealer brokerage firms are responding to the continuing growth in cross-asset relative value trading. For example, as part of inter-dealer brokerage firm GFI's offering, the firm provides a web-based data and analytics platform for cross-asset class analysis, called MarketHub.

"Trading from a cross-asset class perspective has been developing for a while, says Michael Fuhrman, head of e-trading, North America, at GFI. "Through our data and analytics, as well as through our trading systems, we wish to reflect that this is the way traders and investors want to view the world."

MarketHub combines CDS prices with equity prices and equity options pricing. "In future we plan to extend the coverage further – certainly to bonds," says Fuhrman. "There is a vibrant leveraged loan market out there and a good secondary market in loan trading, so loans are a likely second addition, beyond bonds."

Meanwhile, in May 2006, GFI launched a new version of its electronic trading platform, CreditMatch. "We are now combining CDS and cash bonds on the same platform," says GFI's Fuhrman. "That is a first for an inter-dealer brokerage firm. Clients can execute trades for both asset classes. Users see the full range of credit derivatives and also within the same application, all bonds issued by reference entities."

'If you can buy equity put options as a credit hedge cheaper than the relative costs of selling protection, you can monetise the short default risk position – benefiting from positive carry to option maturity'

Stephen Siderow, BlueMountain Capital Management: New derivative products, such as variance, correlation and dividend swaps, provide attractive opportunities to exploit structural mispricings, and to identify and trade relative value and mean-reverting views

In the structured finance credit derivatives space, GFI has been offering brokerage services since the ABX index was launched last year. "There is good activity around the asset-backed index," says Fuhrman.

In the case of debt-equity capital structure arbitrage, the classic trade involves selling credit protection and buying equity options. Theory dictates that corporate bond risk is the equivalent of holding a risk-free bond, plus writing a put option that gives equity holders the right to default, in exchange for transferring ownership of the firm's residual assets to debt holders. Hence, a convergence trade suggests itself if a company's credit derivative spreads look too high compared with the implied equity volatility, or implied volatility looks too low compared with the credit default swap spread.

Notes Tim Backshall, chief credit strategist at independent research boutique Credit Derivatives Research in New York: "If you can buy equity put options as a credit hedge cheaper than the relative costs of selling protection, you can monetise the short default risk position – benefiting from positive carry to option maturity."

Newer innovations in debt-equity capital structure arbitrage and pure equity-related strategies involve equity variance swaps and other instruments. For example, BlueMountain Capital Management recently carved out an equity alternatives fund. The strategy includes credit-equity micro and macro trading, equity dispersion, equity volatility and emerging equity derivatives strategies. Along with equity variance, the fund trades products such as correlation swaps and dividend swaps, and combines these positions with credit derivatives.

Says Stephen Siderow, president, BlueMountain Capital Management: "We have been doing credit-equity and pure equity volatility strategies for well over a year in the flagship fund – BlueMountain Credit Alternatives. We see a lot more opportunities in this space than can be accommodated by the flagship multi-strategy fund.

"New derivative products, such as variance, correlation and dividend swaps, combined with our proprietary data and analytics, provide attractive opportunities to exploit structural mispricings, and to identify and trade relative value and mean-reverting views."

A variance swap is a forward contract on realised variance, or the square of realised volatility. Its payoff is equal to dollar notional x (realised volatility^2 - variance strike price).

The parties agree to make cash payments based on whether the realized variance of a stock or index over a specified period is more or less than an agreed level. The variance buyer receives a payment if the realised variance is higher and receives a payment if it is lower than the agreed level.

Equity variance swaps therefore allow traders to take a "pure" view on the future volatility of a given stock or index. Such swaps allow traders to have a

COMPLEX MARKETS REQUIRE INTELLIGENT SOLUTIONS

INTER-DEALER BROKERAGE

As a major inter-dealer broker in credit and equity markets, GFI specialises in credit and equity default swaps, credit indices, exotic credit structures, OTC and listed equity options, US and European cash equities and a range of other equity derivative instruments.

ONLINE TRADING

CreditMatch® supports the number one broker* in credit default swaps and offers credit traders an STP solution fully integrable with their trade processing and compliant with FpML standards.

MARKETHUB

GFI's MarketHub is a powerful web-based tool for cross asset class analysis. Intuitive analytics, market data and commentary are key for market practitioners looking to take advantage of the equity/credit market correlation.

* Risk Magazine Inter-dealer survey 1998-2005

CONTACT US TODAY
www.GFIgroup.com

constant exposure to volatility, with a fixed gamma and time decay that is not dependent on stock prices.

The BlueMountain fund, which is called BlueMountain Equity Alternatives, includes an equity-credit macro strategy which trades variance swaps on indices, or more tailored baskets of stocks, against credit derivative indices or selected baskets of names. An equity-credit micro strategy applies the strategy to single names.

Michael Fuhrman, GFI: There is a vibrant leveraged loan market out there and a good secondary market in loan trading, so loans are a likely second addition, beyond bonds

Meanwhile, playing the senior and subordinated parts of the unsecured debt capital structure remains a popular arbitrage trade among hedge funds. For example, active credit derivative markets on both a senior and subordinated level exist for European bank issuers. "Strategies such as going long [risk] the subordinated parts of financials, and short [risk] the senior part is an area where we can extract value," says a European-based hedge fund manager trading investment grade credit.

However, it is the extension of single-name credit derivatives trading to the secured part of the debt capital structure that promises significant growth.

Standardised trading terms have emerged in both North America and the European market for single-name default swaps on leveraged loans. However, only the North American standard has found its way into Isda-agreed documentation.

Dealers say liquidity is set to grow off the back of the documentation work in both markets. Ease of access to the leveraged loan class and flexibility of trading are obvious attractions of credit derivatives on loans.

Meanwhile, the use of total return swaps has already greatly extended the involvement of hedge fund managers in the leveraged loan market.

"Institutional non-CLO involvement has grown a lot," says Simon Richards, senior portfolio manager at hedge fund manager RAB Capital, in London. "New financing solutions for loans have been a key to that." RAB Capital manages a long/short European loan fund, launched in 2005.

Historically, prime brokers have not lent against loans, because unlike bonds, loans are not easily transferable. That is obviously a problem for prime brokers from a collateral perspective. The hedge fund buying the loan becomes the lender of record, leaving the prime broker with no direct call on security. Total return swaps, which transfer only economic rights, have been a way around that problem.

The trading flexibility afforded by credit derivatives marks a second phase in the entry of hedge funds into the loan market.

'Institutional non-CLO involvement has grown a lot. New financing solutions for loans have been a key to that'

"Trading credit derivatives on leveraged loans allow us to take positions in names that are not traded in the senior unsecured market," says Jeff Kushner, head of execution at BlueMountain Capital Management. "It offers good scope for relative value trades – senior versus senior unsecured versus equity."

In North America in particular, where loan documentation is more "friendly" towards hedge fund investors, liquidity is predicted to take off.

"The introduction of standardised documentation should significantly boost liquidity," says Lisa Watkinson, global structured credit business development at Lehman Brothers in New York. "Credit derivatives allow easy access to the loan asset class. Relative value trading opportunities include negative basis trades."

Watkinson says that Lehman Brothers is making markets in between 60 and 70 single names in the North American leveraged loan market. Other banks that have been involved early in the development of the market include Credit Suisse, Deutsche Bank, Goldman Sachs, JP Morgan and Morgan Stanley.

The basic trading picture is that leveraged loan credit default swaps should trade tight compared to the loans – at least in benign credit markets where a desire to go short among loan portfolio managers is relatively limited. That is providing opportunities to trade the loan-secured credit default swap basis, and to execute long/short capital structure trades on loan credit derivatives and senior unsecured credit default swaps.

As well as secured loan credit default swaps versus cash loans, traders say that cash loans versus senior unsecured default swaps can be an attractive trade. "Going long loans and short senior unsecured on the same name is a strategy that has done well," says Andrew Feldstein, chief investment officer, BlueMountain Capital Management. "Loan pricing is incredibly rich," he adds, "but relative to bonds they offer opportunities. More liquidity in the high-yield credit derivatives market is making that kind of trade easier."

According to dealers, demand for short protection from correlation desks is adding to the bias towards better loan credit default swap selling.

"Correlation desks are very keen to add new names to their portfolios," says Marcus Schüler, head of integrated credit marketing at Deutsche Bank. "The fact that they now have access to 40 to 50 new exposures [in Europe] is very attractive to them."

Lisa Watkinson, Lehman Brothers: Credit derivatives allow easy access to the loan asset class. Relative value trading opportunities include negative basis trades

Loan portfolio managers may also be tempted to sell protection because of high dollar prices in the loan market. "The default swap is a par instrument so there is no premium at stake if the instrument is called," says Schüler. "Many loans are trading at par, but if the loan is called that premium goes away." He adds: "If we see spread widening, loans could start trading through secured CDS, but currently overall there are more sellers than buyers of protection."

In the European market, leveraged loan credit default swaps have recently been trading some 50bp through cash loans. Towards the start of May, loan credit default swap spreads were on average trading roughly 10bp tighter than their unsecured-implied theoretical value.

Distressed delivers the goods

High-yield funds have been delivering some of the biggest total returns among credit hedge funds. A prime example is the credit hedge fund managed by BlueBay Asset Management.

The firm was established in 2001 by Hugh Willis and Mark Poole – two former co-heads of credit arbitrage trading at JP Morgan in London. BlueBay manages six funds, ranging across investment-grade credit, high-yield credit and emerging markets. Pairs of long-only and long/short funds are managed in each asset case.

In addition, BlueBay has been among the first fund managers to take advantage of new funding techniques at a crossover point with market value CDOs. Unlike rated market value CDOs, such vehicles bypass the public debt market, and instead look to total return swaps and other forms of bank financing.

The BlueBay vehicle, which is called the BlueBay Credit Opportunities fund, was launched in 2005. Citigroup is providing the leverage, which is capped at five times, with a mixture of total return swaps and repos. BlueBay is also involved in structured products, and manages a single-tranche emerging markets CDO.

The firm's Cayman Islands domiciled high-yield total return fund was launched in November 2003. Anthony Robertson, senior portfolio manager, high yield, at BlueBay Asset Management, says that distressed trading was the key to the fund's high return in 2005.

"The distressed market has been the key driver of returns," he says. "The high-yield total return fund made over 17% in 2005. We are seeking good double-digit returns in 2006."

Recapitalisations are a standard part of the fund's distressed investment activity. In addition, BlueBay looks to more private opportunities in the direct lending space.

Says Robertson: "We are involved in buying out significant components of the capital structure, in partnership with others, with a view to recapitalising the business – for example through debt-for-equity swaps.

"In addition, more esoteric single-name opportunities exist. There are interesting opportunities in the loan space, generally sourced from the German bank market."

For hedge funds in the European distressed markets, direct lending, particularly to German Mittelstand companies, has provided an escape route from the crowding in the mainstream market. Traditional distressed opportunities are at a relatively low ebb, but there is plenty of hedge fund liquidity pushing up prices.

The scaling back of relationships between German SMEs and their main lenders – the German Landesbanks – is providing new investment opportunities.

Says Robertson: "Lending relationships are slowly shifting, as the Landesbanks adjust to new commercial realities. As a result, opportunities exist, but on a highly selective basis."

Meanwhile, the distressed cycle is due for a more dynamic phase, as the current period of high leverage multiples for LBOs starts to supply new broken credits. The simple fact that the LBO market has grown enormously in size suggests there will be a bumper crop.

BlueBay's long-only high-yield bond fund, which is benchmarked against the Merrill Lynch European currencies high-yield constrained index, returned 10.53% in 2005.

Chapter 4
stampeding into value:
structured credit
relative value trading

Dealers say that there is more capital at work in the credit correlation market today than at any previous stage in the market's development. That should not come as any surprise given the value opportunities that have followed from the repricing in correlation in 2005.

The shift in value into equity tranches and the emergence of new plays at the super-senior level has produced investor interest up and down the capital structure. Also, the development of a term structure in the tranche market – itself a product of the dislocation in 2005 – has resulted in active curve trading, and has greatly extended the range of combinations for tranche relative value trading.

As part of curve-based strategies, forward-starting trades are in vogue, reflecting steep curve shapes. Other relative value strategies include trading the different series of the standard index tranches, to capture mispricings due to portfolio composition changes.

Trading of lower detachment points on index tranches, reflecting the fact that standard first-loss tranches no longer attach close to the expected loss in the underlying index, has also attracted hedge fund interest.

However, many dealers appear to have pulled back from making markets in so-called tranchelets, due to lack of pricing uniformity.

Although the opportunities to trade relative value have never been greater, the correlation market remains highly technical, reflecting the impact of dealer hedging activity.

For hedge funds mindful of the volatility in May 2005, this has encouraged a shift towards longer lock-ups for the correlation funds they manage. Lock-up periods can today be as long as seven or 10 years for standalone funds. Meanwhile, a useful by-product of credit CPPI is that it helps keep funds locked up.

London-based credit investment managers Cheyne Capital and Cairn Capital have both launched managed correlation strategies using a credit CPPI format over the past year. CPPI provides leveraged exposure combined with a guaranteed return of capital.

Meanwhile, North American credit hedge fund managers that are said to

'Structured credit long-short strategies used to be more exclusively a hedge fund type play. But there has been a huge increase in other types of investors who are open to the idea and happy to take positions in long/short tranche trades'

be making the most of the strong interest from investors in credit correlation include Citadel Investment Group. The hedge fund manager has been in the correlation market for some time, trading correlation strategies as part of a multi-strategy credit hedge fund.

"The correlation repricing was a bit of a catharsis," notes one North American credit correlation trader. "Today you have more stable capital left in the market. Citadel, for example, has a very stable investor base."

Meanwhile, BlueMountain Capital Management has launched no fewer than five standalone correlation funds since summer 2005. The first of these pursues a non-delta hedged long equity tranche strategy, but with scope for single-name hedging. A follow-up fund pursues the same strategy. Meanwhile, a fund called Timberline follows a delta-hedged long correlation strategy. The final fund – BlueCorr – is an actively traded vehicle, taking long and short positions across the CDO capital structure and term structure.

The value that can be captured in the tranche market is today encouraging

Options on options

Options on tranches are making a tentative appearance in the market, according to dealers, but are likely to appeal only to the brave-hearted. "Tranche valuation is now quite standard, and certainly it is possible to write options on tranches," notes one trader. "However, it remains a frontier trade. There is already an option-like feature in tranches, so it is like options on options.

"On the other hand, CDS options on the unleveraged indices is very linear, and very liquid."

He adds: "It is still relatively simple strategies for trading [flow] index options. The market is very liquid but we are not at the stage of the rates market, where you can have five or six different option legs to the trade. The newer strategies involve taking a view on volatility over time and trading different maturities of options against one another."

Hedge funds have been happy to come in and sell volatility in large size. "Strategies that are positive carry tend to be popular," says a London-based options trader. "Selling volatility and having a premium upfront is tempting."

But single-name options look unlikely to gain much traction. Says Eric Lepage, Calyon's global head of structured credit trading and quantitative research: "Trading single-name credit options raises various issues. There is the liquidity of the underlying. If you want to do clean gamma management on hedging strategies, there is a cost.

"There is also the question of the jumpiness of single-name credit default swap spreads, especially for deep out-of-the-money options. Plus, if we start having a market, all the corporate issuers will probably be looking forward to buying default- and-out options on themselves. This could push dealers to short some gamma on single-name credit options in big size."

Expanding was the least we could do to connect you to the major worldmarkets

Calyon is the Corporate and Investment Bank of the Crédit Agricole Group,
combining the businesses of Crédit Agricole Indosuez and Crédit Lyonnais' Corporate
and Investment Banking division. A major player in Europe, Calyon enjoys
a global coverage (60 countries), a full range of products and services,
and strong ratings (AA- Standard & Poor's, Aa2 Moody's, AA FitchRatings).
Over 1,800 Capital Markets experts deployed in 30 dealing rooms will
help you find the best solution to attain your goals.
This is why, we strive to remain your privileged partner.

CALYON
CORPORATE AND INVESTMENT BANK
GROWING TO MATCH YOUR GROWTH

www.calyon.com

CRÉDIT AGRICOLE GROUP

Eric Lepage, Calyon: Correlation is now more demystified, as a result of education, the greater availability of pricing models, and consensus about using base correlation for quoting implied correlation

many other investors besides hedge funds to put on trades. For example, bank investors are actively taking on long/short positions.

Says Eric Lepage, global head of structured credit trading and quantitative research at Calyon: "Structured credit long-short strategies used to be more exclusively a hedge fund type play. But there has been a huge increase in other types of investors who are open to the idea and happy to take positions in long/short tranche trades. That can be done synthetically or in funded format, and combined with capital protection."

Adds Lepage: "Correlation is now more demystified, as a result of education, the greater availability of pricing models, and consensus about using base correlation for quoting implied correlation."

Equity tranche plays involving protection selling on initial names to default in a broad basket, versus protection buying on initial names to default in a risky sub-basket, is one type of long/short strategy that has gained some traction.

"We have done quite a lot of long and short combinations like that," says Calyon's Lepage. "It gives investors attractive positive carry. It is an attractive trade for hedge funds as well as other types of investor."

An example of this trade might involve a basket of 60 or so credits, the majority of them rated triple A to single A, and the remainder rated low double B or single B.

The investor sells protection on the first names to default – for example, the first two defaults. For the other part of the trade, the investor buys protection on the first defaults in the basket of names rated low double B and single B.

The trade can be structured to provide an investment-grade rating, with a positive carry.

"The short position reduces the expected loss, which allows you to achieve an investment-grade rating for the overall structure," says Ally Chow, head of structured credit product management and syndicate at Calyon. There is limited risk on default, she notes. "The investor bears losses only if the credits are rated single A or above default, while at the same time credits rated low double B or lower do not default," she says.

Variations on the trade could involve going short protection on a thin equity piece, and long protection on a mezzanine sub-basket of the same portfolio.

"First-to-default or i-to-j-to-default versus tranches are solutions we

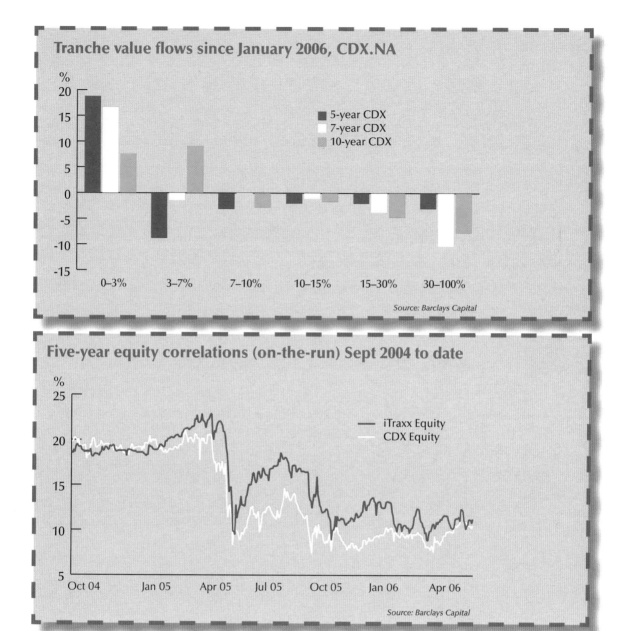

Tranche value flows since January 2006, CDX.NA

Legend:
- 5-year CDX
- 7-year CDX
- 10-year CDX

X-axis: 0–3%, 3–7%, 7–10%, 10–15%, 15–30%, 30–100%

Source: Barclays Capital

Five-year equity correlations (on-the-run) Sept 2004 to date

Legend:
- iTraxx Equity
- CDX Equity

X-axis: Oct 04, Jan 05, Apr 05, Jul 05, Oct 05, Jan 06, Apr 06

Source: Barclays Capital

provide as part of a broad menu of tailor-made structures," says Calyon's Lepage.

"For example, we also trade a significant amount of complex basket with non-linear pay off to recovery, as well as bespoke versus index tranches. Index tranches are liquid and transparent, but you are compelled to keep to that basket or roll it. With a self-managed transaction, the manager is able to do substitutions and keep a non-barbelled portfolio if they are wanting to trade equity tranches."

One trade that has gathered momentum, in a period of steep curves, is the forward starting CDO. These transactions are quasi long/short trades, in which the investor's exposure to losses begins at a future starting point.

Forward-starting trades are in vogue, reflecting steep curve shapes. Other relative value strategies include trading the different series of the standard index tranches, to capture mispricings due to portfolio composition changes

Thus, a five-year starting in two-year CDO is the equivalent of a seven-year long CDO with offsetting short positions for the first two years. Typically the implicit short position is for the first two years of the trade.

Steep credit curves have created the arbitrage for the trade, as spread levels for forward credit default swaps have more than compensated for the cost of the implicit short position over the early part of the transaction.

Typically, trades are structured so that the investor receives Libor flat or a spread over Libor over the first part of the trade, and a credit-related spread once the exposure to default risk starts. Alternatively, the same premium can be spread across the life of the transaction, from trade date to maturity.

"In our structure, you get paid a guaranteed coupon of Libor plus x, followed by a credit-related spread," says Chow at Calyon in London. "We have also shown deals without the Libor element, but a Libor-related coupon suits clients such as banks who need to cover their funding cost."

Typically if defaults occur over the first part of the forward-starting CDO, the size of the portfolio diminishes as reference entities drop out. However, the dollar size of the tranche and its subordination remains constant, resulting in increased subordination in percentage terms.

"Some structures allow for replenishment," says Chow, "but typically the portfolio gets smaller and the transaction gets less leveraged as names are taken out."

Chapter 5
time to talk alpha:
portable alpha strategies

Credit hedge funds are high-powered alpha-generating machines – at least according to the marketing literature. So it should follow that long/short funds are a natural home for portable alpha strategies.

Portable alpha – the technique of grafting unrelated alpha-generating strategies onto an investment manager's core market exposure – is certainly being applied more and more in credit. And credit hedge funds are benefiting from that flow. However, some firms say there are also arguments for directing portable alpha strategies towards predominantly long-only vehicles, rather than full-blown long/short vehicles.

For example, that is the approach that has been adopted by fixed-income investment management firm BlueBay Asset Management. The firm runs both long/short and long-only credit and emerging market funds, and is pushing a portable alpha business in its long-only vehicles – particularly its high-yield and emerging market credit funds.

"Many absolute return products contain hidden beta," says Linda Lysell, joint head of structured products at BlueBay Asset Management in London. "For example, leveraged hedge funds with a floating-rate base return plus alpha target often incorporate beta risk in the alpha component. BlueBay's long-only approach to portable alpha produces what is, in our view, a 'true' absolute return."

Portable alpha strategies work by separating out the alpha and beta components of the core market exposure and alpha-generating strategy, typically by using index futures or total return swaps, and through use of passive tracker funds. The beta, or market return from the investment manager's designated benchmark, is retained, and the selected value-generating strategy provides the alpha, or risk-adjusted excess return.

Demand from investors for juicier returns – particularly from pension funds facing funding shortfalls – has driven the move into portable alpha. Such strategies give an implicit thumbs-down to traditional long-only styles of asset management, by allowing investors to target manager skills away from their core strategies.

The risk, of course, is that the alpha-generating strategy doesn't deliver.

'Alpha strategies work best where markets are inefficient. Asset classes like emerging markets and European high-yield credit can offer significant alpha potential'

Smart tailoring

Fund derivatives are a valuable tool for hedge funds and other investment managers in the all-important business of attracting fund inflows. Fund derivatives are commonly used to give investors access to funds which they are restricted from investing in directly. For instance, if an investor cannot invest in an unrated fund, fund derivatives allow the creation of special purpose vehicle to invest in the fund, paying the investor a rated note.

Fund derivatives are also used to create customised risk return profiles, such as principal protection. For example, principal protection on BlueBay Asset Management's funds is provided through Barclays' investment banking platform. "In the past two years we have done a lot of principal-protected business in Asia and in Japan in particular," says BlueBay's joint head of structured products, Linda Lysell. "For us this is a globally marketed product."

Adds Lysell: "In the past it has mostly been banks offering principal protection on funds of funds, but less on single-manager or single-strategy risk. Today there are a lot more investment banks in this area, people have grown better at evaluating the risk, and there is a much greater willingness to offer principal protection linked to an individual fund."

Principal protection in the form of a fixed-income note creates beneficial regulatory capital treatment, which is therefore attractive for banks and insurance companies, says BlueBay's structured products co-head, Wei Foong Lee. The fixed-income notes can be structured to pay a regular fixed or performance-related coupon or, instead of principal protection, a high guaranteed coupon. That can be attractive for insurance companies and pension funds looking for assets with regular income, says Lee, but also potential for capital appreciation.

"It's also possible to have additional leverage," he says. "Barclays could provide additional funding as part of the note structure, and charge a competitive funding rate. For example, depending on the currency and maturity of the note, it could potentially be linked to 200% exposure to the fund."

BlueBay's principal protection business applies to its long-only funds, but the firm is also in the process of extending it to the long/short funds. "That is still in discussion at the moment, but will be launched shortly," says Lee.

Fund derivatives provide a major benefit by keeping mandates simple for the funds, adds Lee. "Different investors have different requirements," he says, "but rather than manage a lot of segregated managed accounts with varying investment guidelines, we try to offer structured products that are linked to the existing BlueBay funds.

"Derivatives of the funds offer investors bespoke solutions with different structural features from a direct credit fund investment, while allowing our portfolio managers to concentrate their efforts on managing only the existing funds."

However, BlueBay Asset Management argues that portable alpha strategies work best where markets are inefficient. "Asset classes like emerging markets and European high-yield credit can offer significant alpha potential," says Wei Foong Lee, joint head of structured products at BlueBay. "Our emerging market and high-yield long-only funds have produced gross annualised alpha of 4.56% and 4.6%, respectively, since 2002 to the end of April 2006."

Although categorised as long-only funds, BlueBay's vehicles in fact have some flexibility to go short using credit derivatives. The firm says that the ability to manage risk from the short side is integral to the ability to generate consistently good risk-adjusted excess returns.

The long-only vehicles are Luxembourg-listed Ucits (Part 1) funds, and can use up to 15% of the net assets of the portfolio to go short individual names or credit indices using credit derivatives.

"The funds make use of a more extensive tool-kit than traditional long-only funds," says Lysell. "They are very actively managed by traditional standards."

The simplest approach to portable alpha is to replace an allocation to an actively managed long-only fund with a passive strategy, and make a capital allocation to another strategy generating 'pure alpha'. That is the ideal scenario, as there is no overlapping or unwanted beta to worry about. However, the challenge is to find an alpha strategy that has no hidden beta – in other words, is genuinely market neutral.

An alternative approach, as advocated by firms such as BlueBay, is to select a long-only alpha provider, isolate the alpha, and transfer it to the investor's chosen benchmark.

Linda Lysell, BlueBay Asset Management: many absolute return products contain hidden beta. For example, leveraged hedge funds with a floating-rate base return plus alpha target often incorporate beta risk in the alpha component

However, the snag with relative-return high-yield and emerging market credit funds is that the beta is not easily stripped out, as liquid futures contracts do not exist on the benchmark indices. However, a recent initiative by BlueBay, in conjunction with UBS, aims to separate the alpha and beta components of the firm's funds without the need for complex structuring and derivatives.

The approach involves offloading the beta returns from the funds to one set of investors, and giving the alpha to another set, thereby sidestepping the problem of how to actively short the beta.

"UBS buys our fund units so they are long both the beta and the alpha," says Lee. "Our benchmark is quoted daily but not liquidly traded, so you cannot go short the benchmark easily like you can with an equity index. One solution

'You can go out to investors who just want to receive the beta returns, and provide the alpha to another set, although this would require an investment banking partner with the distribution breadth to access these different investor types'

would be to construct a portfolio of bonds and actively short each component of the benchmark. Or, more simply, you can go out to investors who just want to receive the beta returns, and provide the alpha to another set, although this would require an investment banking partner with the distribution breadth to access these different investor types."

Adds Lee: "An investor might come in and want Libor plus alpha. Or they might demand inflation plus leveraged alpha, or an index tracker fund with an alpha overlay and principal protection. There are many variations which we can offer and we are seeing quite a bit of interest from around the world."

Says Lee: "Adding US dollar Libor to alpha in the region of 4.6% gives you an 8% return product. If on top of that you add leverage – say Libor plus three times alpha – you could see double-digit returns."

Lee says that beta investors may also find it attractive to receive the beta from the BlueBay funds – such as the JP Morgan EMBI Global Diversified – instead of paying a fee for a traditional index tracking fund with potential tracking errors.

BlueBay says it has done over $200 million in portable alpha business. "We have done over $100 million in Japan and Asia ex-Japan as well as a few big European trades," says Lee.

UK and Australian pension funds are two key markets that BlueBay would like to tap in future for portable alpha business. However, progress there will depend on pension fund consultancies getting on board.

Chapter 6
handling succession:
event risk trading

Trading of LBO and M&A risk was supposed to be easy money for credit hedge funds in the first part of 2006. A hyperactive rumour mill, in Europe at least, resulted in surging volumes in names that had previously rarely been traded. But that was before credit derivatives documentation spoilt the party.

The limitations of Isda's successor event language have been well documented. The language governs what happens to existing credit derivative contracts when one entity succeeds to the obligations of another. Lawyers who drafted the documentation say it achieves clarity, because it is not an all-embracing attempt to cover situations where successor problems can occur.

But its focus on the transfer of existing debt between reference entities leaves some gaping holes. Leveraged acquisitions can involve the target company's debt being bought back, and new debt being issued at a new holding company. Similarly, capital reorganisations can result in new holding companies issuing all the new debt, leaving protection buyers stranded once debt matures at the old reference entity.

Despite these limitations, credit hedge funds involved in event risk trading say that the strategy is still due to deliver good returns in 2006. "Event-driven credit investment will very much be a key for performance," says a portfolio manager at a London-based credit hedge fund who declined to be named. "Name selection is key. In the middle of February, it was LBO euphoria. That was replaced by panic over the successor mechanism. People will realise that they have been too aggressively focused on the successor issue. These situations are in fact rare. It will not occur across the board."

Adds another credit hedge fund manager: "To a certain extent problems around succession language might affect liquidity, but it is a risk that can be quantified. It's important to take it name by name. It is also the case that this sort of thing provides people with some of the volatility that gives them returns. However, fund managers will be making sure they are entirely aware of the risks they might be running."

Strategies for trading leveraged M&A situations have come in a variety of flavours. The smartest trade has been to buy change of control bonds and buy

'To a certain extent problems around succession language might affect liquidity, but it is a risk that can be quantified. It's important to take it name by name'

credit default swap protection. If a buy-out takes place, bank lenders will want everything that is inside the tenor of the loan bought out. Event risk trades also get expressed using curve steepeners, or by selling index protection to fund short positions in baskets of likely LBO candidates.

Considerable resources have been devoted to the trade. Financial models have been in overdrive spitting out lists of the most likely M&A targets on which to go long protection. The prospect of capturing spreads movements of a magnitude of 200bp or more makes event risk trades hard to ignore.

Says Mahesh Bhimalingam, credit strategist at Barclays Capital: "All other things being equal, there are good returns to be made if the investor guesses the LBO candidate correctly. Take the case of a fairly innocent-looking company with good money streams and not much debt. Credit default swaps on the name could be trading at around 45bp to 55bp. Suddenly there is an LBO rumour and the credit spreads gap out to 100bp to 150bp. As talks are seen to progress this could widen further to 200bp to 250bp. Should the LBO actually happen spreads could end up at 250bp to 300bp. Clearly, if you get the call right at any stage you will stand to profit."

Because spreads are so tight, credit hedge funds have viewed going long protection on event risk names as a cheap option. That view changed when spreads were crushed tighter in March. Notes one credit hedge fund manager: "The short might look cheap, but not when spreads on names trading at 40bp to 60bp collapse. That doesn't look like cheap insurance. A slow grinding in of spreads isn't good either. Every day that spreads go tighter you drop a bit of P&L."

Paying protection premium and playing a waiting game has at times been frustrating. Dealers say that leveraged M&A activity has been lower than expected so far in 2006.

Things came to a head in March, when hedging activity in the structured credit market coincided with waning confidence in event risk trades in the European market.

"The trade was starting to die a death. There was no back-up to any of the rumours – they didn't come to much," says a London-based hedge fund manager. "At the same time, we had a lot of synthetic CDO issuance that forced CDS spreads tighter. Everyone got squeezed. A lot of people possibly lost some of the money they had made by picking LBO possibilities."

In the North American market, event risk trading has been more level-headed. "In Europe it was crazy," says a US observer. "It was a rumour a day. But there have also been good opportunities here. Jones Apparel is a good example. There we started putting on selective shorts at the middle of last year. We did very well on that trade."

According to a European trader, panic surrounding pest control company Rentokil, around the March roll date, set the short squeeze in motion. "Rentokil led to a capitulation in the single-name market," he says.

Traders twigged that once the last outstanding bonds at Rentokil Initial 1927 matured, existing derivative contracts would be without deliverables. A capital reorganisation, in 2005, added a new top parent company, Rentokil Initial, to the capital structure. Bonds issued this year by Rentokil Initial are guaranteed by Rentokil Initial 1927. However, that guarantee ceases when the bonds at Rentokil Initial 1927 mature. All the bank debt is held at Rentokil Initial, leaving protection buyers stranded.

A few weeks earlier, bond buybacks by Colt Telecom and UK retailer Sainsbury had already set the tone, resulting in successor-event driven rallies in both credits. "Those were trades that looked like no-brainers," says a credit derivatives trader in London. "Everybody was short Sainsbury. The curve collapsed."

Meanwhile, UK glassmaker Pilkington was being actively traded back and forth, when the Rentokil bombshell dropped. Pilkington was unlikely to fall foul of succession language, suggesting some European traders of LBO names have got their homework cut out. A few weeks later, there was panic trading in Air France – another unlikely successor victim.

Mahesh Bhimalingam, Barclays Capital: All other things being equal, there are good returns to be made if the investor guesses the LBO candidate correctly

Pilkington is being acquired by Nippon Sheet Glass. Volatility in the name related to whether upstream guarantees would apply, if Pilkington's debt was bought back. Assuming a debt buyback, lack of upstream guarantees from Pilkington to the lenders at NSG UK would rule out a successor event.

"People were getting into a frenzy," notes one buy-side trader. "I received a Bloomberg heading from a colleague asking 'can CDS go negative?'"

There was no explicit mention by NSG of a guarantee – because of financial assistance rules. "People were so worried," he adds, "but it was simply down to UK legislation. While you have the tender for the company no upstream guarantee is allowed."

Although US trading of M&A names has been somewhat more sedate, the market has also been grappling with succession language. For example, Ford's tender last year for the outstanding bonds issued by rentals firm Hertz sent Hertz credit protection tighter by 100bp. The bond tender formed part of Ford's divestiture of Hertz, a wholly owned subsidiary, to a private equity group.

The original plan had been for Ford to exchange a portion of Hertz's debt with Ford Motor Credit. That would have qualified as a successor event, resulting in existing Hertz credit derivative contracts being split equally between Hertz and Ford Motor Credit.

US travel giant Cendant triggered successor-related trading, in March, due to a bond buyback and issuance of new debt as part of a demerger.

In the wake of these trading debacles, perhaps it is not surprising that Isda says it is working on new succession language. But credit derivatives lawyers concede that it will be impossible to capture all scenarios using a reworked successor event mechanism.

"It is difficult to eliminate these situations, because companies are going to continue to restructure and change their form, and in a variety of ways," says Willem Sels, credit strategist at Dresdner Kleinwort Wasserstein. "Corporate actions by their nature are surprising and not easy to predict."

In the meantime, many funds are likely to continue to see a compelling case for going short event risk names. The profit potential is too big to ignore.